Penny Ante Feud 14

The Fires of Earth

Shoe
Music
Press

Penny Ante Feud 14: The Fires of Earth is published by Shoe Music Press, Alpharetta, GA USA. Its contents are protected by copyright law where applicable.

Cover image: *Woman in cell, playing solitaire* by Nickolas Muray c. 1950 in the Public Domain.

Penny Ante Feud has appeared in serial under ISSN: 2153-6422.

Email us at shoemusicpress@gmail.com and visit us online at www.shoemusicpress.com

Elena Botts

my mind is on raindrops.

she's drunk on lake water,
piss and frog liver,
her head smoked up in
burn-out masochism,
embers of self-depreciation.
tombstone teeth buried in gums
where she fed her fingers to frustration,
warm bloody things.
we waved hello again,
smiling because dreams are
immediate and reality
is nothing.

Bruce Deitrick Price

Femme Fatality

in my arms
she is on guard,
firing into shadows:
she lives with the safety
off

her beauty is full of shock
and blood,
limping back from battles
on the far side of affection

in her wary eyes
I can see that
each day is a minefield
which she clears
with great loss of life

high in her voice I hear
ack-ack, red and black
like furious flowers
indignant above the injured land

at night she curls up
in her wounds
and sleeps the sleep
of the unburied dead

Holly Day

The Photographs Tell the Story

I was the only one who survived, a child
surrounded by the corpses of my family. I hid
in the rocks until the seagulls came.
I still have nightmares about
all the blood.

Afterwards, a photographer took me in,
said it was the least he could do
considering I had made his career. He took pictures
of me at the crime scene, the first day,
a year later,
years later, as a fully-functioning
adult.

When I was able,
I left his company,
became a bird trainer at the zoo. The soft, warm feathers
of the birds remind me of my mother,
their black eyes remind me of my father.
I feel at home here, inside these cages,
devoid of floodlights
and casting couches.

Grief

Your mother in a pink dress will marry for the third time.
She searches for her mascara in the deep seat of a chair
and finds a little boy dripping egg on the upholstery.
Your brother slips on marbles, tiny planets on the floor.
In the dark
all you see is the red tip of the cigarette burning
and know at the other end
is your father.
And now your mother in the green lawn chair
waves through the dark
to a friend,
you and your brother
ride bikes
through heavy summer air.

You are standing at the edge of it.
Everything you have ever had and lost.

Why must we always lose our
warm cloth mothers,
our up-standing fathers,
must our sun-baked childhoods
turn dry and wear out?
Can't we keep our special
pocket knife
our glowing

4

front-tooth-missing smiles,
our bangs chopped off, uneven
scabs on both knees,
mosquito bites?
Why must even these graces
be swept away?

Violeta Y. Valdes

Untitled

I am afraid of today.
With its white sea of uncertainty.
I debate if I should leave now or wait.
If I lose control, I might just slip away.
Nothing is ever guaranteed.

If I stay, I will lay motionless losing my mind.
The price to pay for not entertaining time.

The cold is a bitter challenge.
Never take it for granted unless you are prepared.
Prepared to suffer all its delicious damage.
Its invitation to sleep a gentle sleep.
I tried my best to venture out.
I should have stayed in my bed.
Then I could have tried again.

JD DeHart

Morsel

Pardon me the eater declared
Before the evening meal was complete
Shoveling the food in mass droves
The morsel a small matter
Barely observed, washed down
Crushed with uneven molars
Swallowed whole with a gulp
Expendable
What must it be to exist
As that bit of sustenance
Sliding down the throat
Molded by rolling acids
Malleable
Absorbed into the stream
Even into the mind
Suddenly animating hands and feet.

Peter Victor

Self Portrait

With a contradiction
Is how
It begins
Reaching deep
Into
Days
Hours
And lives
Flashing by
Some lives lost
Loves lost
While others
Remain in flower

Now
There are bits and pieces of you
All over these pages
Now
I will love you forever
Hope you don't mind
Of course
It doesn't matter if you do
That is the beautiful thing
About wanting nothing
Or as they say in the field
Nothingness

Let's go back further
The brothers at sea
Yelling
"Do you hearrrr ME!"
Some comments are never forgotten
"He's no normal white man
He might be some kind of fucked up
Canadian white man
But he's no normal white man."
If they only knew
I will tell the truth now
There wasn't a ghost in my room
But...
I enjoyed the rapt attention
Of course
I neglected to mention
I replaced the dead guy
I know
Everybody knows
You guys killed him
And, I will tell you now fellas
That guy did not have to die
I cannot say he shouldn't have
I do not know that
Only
He did not have to
He had a wife...children
The FBI was asking me about it

(Continued on page 10)

In my room
"What do you know?"
They looked at Storm's photo
"What a beautiful dog."
I wanted to say…
Do you think
I do not see through your childish ploy
To get me talking
Telling you what I have figured out
Over a five-month sea voyage
I can tell you now
It almost worked
I have always been a fool
When it comes to talking about my dogs

Another comment

"This is how they do you in the pen."
As he played with his belt buckle in the bright sunlight
I sat on an overturned five-gallon bucket
Looking on – wheels turning – while waiting for the pilot
I guess in the sunlight and silence
We both knew
He was looking into his future

Yet another comment

"Bos'n, you cannot do this on your own
You need a friend."

Enter Charles
Charles and I would sit up on the bow
Beneath a canopy of stars
In the middle of the wide open deep ocean
Making way
Smoking
And talking about stuff
He was my friend
Sitting at the dock in New Orleans
I yelled at him across decks
"Charles, I am walking to the store
Be back in an hour."
He looked at me – we locked eyes
And he slowly shook his head

Let's jump up here again and move back further
She stood facing the window
Slowly taking off her shirt
Reaching behind her she undid the clasp
All fell to the floor
She slowly turned around
Revealing
The one-quarter inch thick fresh scar that ran from just above her naval
Up between her breasts
To a spot a couple inches below her throat
She softly touched the spot between her breasts while looking at me
"It's no good."
But, this is all becoming sad

(Continued on page 12)

Here give me your hand
Let's go back yet further

"Stop!"
Now this!
Is one of my favorite spots!
The overturned boats on the beach
Muffling our laughs into each others shoulders as we listen to couples
Walking by in the night
I know there is someone
On the other side of the pond
Probably reading these words
Laughing
While saying, "OH MY GAWD!"

Some lives lost
Loves lost
While others remain in flower
We are moving forward now
Some things
Take a long time to grow
I never would have believed
How long
And others
Shoot...
They just never take hold
One of my favorite quotes
Of all time
Magic Johnson

After being told he had tested positive
For the AIDS virus
Shoot
"Things be that way sometimes."

BZ Niditch

Jazz Violinist

Minding my own business
being shy for the cameras
on way to my gig
walking over this metropolis
without an attaché case
only this cold luggage
like my pawned violin
held by four strings
containing a life's work
of quartets, riffs
and songs for our time
with vital plays on words
a cup of java in one hand
and a murdered Danish
in the other
shaking off a coffee cup
with schnapps
on a Southern road
in a runaway midnight
of a day
such as this,
you may not yet recognize
the composer inside him
in his all black cape.

John N. Miller

The Shell Collector

"I had not known death had undone so many."
—T.S. Eliot, "The Waste Land"

My alter ego. I have seen him
stooped, head bowed, hands joined behind his back,
scanning the tide-line of an island beach
for the external skeletons
of gastropods and bivalves.
                                              Death
is multitudinous at certain depths
Most of his scallops, augers,
conches, cones, cowries, whelks,
murexes, periwinkles, lettered olives,
striped bubble shells and wentletraps
had lost once-living innards.
Churned from their reef and sea-floor charnels
in the tumult of waves cresting,
curling, smashing against shore,
some few survived intact
                                      like caskets
in a cemetery
after saturation bombings.

I have watched him pick from the detritus
and dried seaweed something

(Continued on page 16)

15

wind and waves and tide together
tossed up from the ocean bed
unbroken, a bone-white memento mori.

Like him, I've knelt by tidal pools
to prey on hermits lodged in vacant shells
of recently dead sea snails—if collected,
buried alive before they stank.

Years ago, emerging from the mist
that shrouded a rain forest on O'ahu,
he met me after having hunted land shells,
the bright-ringed outer skeletons of snails
that fed on mountain mulberry leaves
I too had been scrutinizing.
We compared finds, mine more multi-colored,
but his, he claimed, more valuable
because less common. Neither of us knew
their death could undo an entire species
as collectors' items—
remnant, empty, fragile, faded shells
under glass in a museum.

Salvatore Marici

My Cousin Anthony

The CEO of a real estate mutual fund
dresses in a black tailored suit
at his nephew's wedding.
As we watch
white people dance
to rap he says,
I drive
from my Michigan Avenue condo
to work instead of walking.
It saves 9 minutes.
You cannot buy back time.

This Sunday
the government credits
this millionaire one hour
in the name of saving daylight.
In 60 minutes,
he reads prospectuses, selects stocks
his company will buy and sell
then sips a single malt. He bought
6.7 commutes
with his interest free loan.

Joseph Stern

Civility

I step into a vanilla restaurant
To eat with my eyes
And start chewing on the waiter
Who is coming with some tenderizer.

He begins with an artificial flavor
In crunching a query through his teeth
And I tell him I'll climb a vodka on the rocks
And make it tall cause I'm thirsty for a change of music.

So he withdraws
While sprouting garnish and spouting it
With puffery into a bunch of crockery
So I sharp eye him a skewer:

Enough with kneading dough,
Play your meat straight and bring me my drink.
Then, with a deliberate sauce,
I ask him to etc. it over and please thank you.

So when the waiter jaunts back with my vodka
He uncorks the specials in a translucid tone
Of vegetative calmness
With a manipulative dressing of very salty syllables.

And, with a caustic bow,
He tells me to order my expectations
By the number. And he'll return.
So I sit with my music and ponder my choices,

Hearing the overhead fan as it spins *hello*, *hello* and *hello*,
And I tell it thank you for the softer touch,
And I'll try not to stare at your pole dance,
Hoping at least that can pass for table manners.

Annika Reitenga

Prism

Meaning: I am master here.
Popping little yellow circles in my mouth.
Pour   way down my throat   vodka.
Dressed in pale skin. Naked under the sheets.
Sometimes he's aggressive   gotta hold on me.
Never let me go, my internal dialogue.
By Sunday he's forgotten my name though.
I stay home washing off his scent. Smooth jazz in the bath.
Saxophone sailing over bubbles.
Soap scrubs my skin. Hot to touch.
Like the iron sitting dangerously close to the tub.

Most sex induces.
Remember the trip in the summer. The sunburn's sting.
The soft hands grazing your hips   then down lower
Smooth stomach muscles flex. Sand everywhere.
You still feel its rough touch. All night
You were taken hostage by salt and soft waves.
Dirty money. Bite your tongue. Shield your conscience.
His warm body told you it was okay.
His grip could fix everything.
High in paradise city.

Longing, what is that?
I'll scream your name. Beg you not to disappear.
Hold me like a python.

20

I'll watch you like a tiger. Green eyes. Claws meant for holding.
I've been meaning to capture you when no one is around.
Hold you for ransom.
You've got a body worth a million dollars
And some gold coins.
With you attraction comes naturally.
Day and night. Give up the fight.
I'm waiting in your garden come outside.

Desire, what is that?
Beer slips down my body. Deeper.
It's strong on my tongue. Smooth in my throat.
Craddle my neck like an infant. I crave the tenderness.
Only for a moment. Then explode. Steamy and mad.
I need the mayhem. The contradictions.
Fall asleep next to me. Still and calm.
A body stiff beside me.

Fabulous things, stars.
I sigh under the blackness. Let it escape my skeleton.
Out into orbit.
You stay content. A simple being. Satisfied within minutes.
Easy to navigate. I let you cross my mind before I drift off.
Breaths slowing down.
Heartbeat not so frantic.
Eyelids limp on eyeballs.
I loosen.
Into dreamworld with you.

Nicholas R. Larche

The Ole Clapboard

The ole clapboard house
on dusty Mine Road
stands in proffer of spite.

The lives of those
who've resided betwixt
the stump and barbwire
speak of nothing new.

The chimney whittled of its dignity,
the tin rust and rued,
only the floorboards of tradition abide.

Unsalvageable mechanics
buried half-deep.

A time when life was measured
in winters survived.

Bobbi Sinha-Morey

The Girl Upstairs

The girl upstairs is busy
entertaining again; I wish
I could set my clock by
the footfall on the stairs.
I often see her, coming
and going on the stairs
or running off to the
market. Sometimes late
at night I hear her playing
sad music or walking
overhead. In the daytime
she smiles, but not at me.

April Mae M. Berza

Mornings and Mournings

The soul of loneliness envelops our mornings
That we fill it with our own solitude,
The loneliness of soul envelops our mournings.

We seek the pulse of thunders and lightnings
In the vast universe filled with gratitude,
The soul of loneliness envelops our mornings.

The wind commiserates with the fledglings
Along with the elders in their fortitude,
The loneliness of soul envelops our mournings.

When the being abandoned its belongings,
Our world is divided into multitudes;
The soul of loneliness envelops our mornings.

Witnessing the flapping of full-pledged wings
Of our dreams that are bare and nude,
The loneliness of soul envelops our mournings.

Sorrow travels in our veins and brings
The art of pain as pain in art already queued;
The soul of loneliness envelops our mornings,
The loneliness of soul envelops our mournings.

Andrew Weston

Virtual Reality

Amid the bronchial harmony of coughing and wheezing,
Psychotic grumbling,
And rancid broken pipes endlessly dripping a staccato beat,
Cardboard boxes congregate.

A virtual city,
Spread across the suburbs of stairwells and basement delivery chutes,
Hidden in plain sight beneath our feet.

Piss-stained distilleries
Of body odor, vomit,
And lice-infested notoriety,
Where the heady bouquet of ammonia,
Connects at an unerring level with fomenting trash.
Both hum to an insect chorus,
A genesis of mutated exigency.

In darkened corners,
Where fetid, greasy puddles stagnate,
A corpse lies rotting.
Putrid, forgotten,
Picked clean of anything of value
Long ago,
And discarded to the evolution of its own decay.

(Continued on page 26)

(Continued from page 25)

Gnawed extremities
Give evidence of rats at play,
Ancient plague carriers
Replaced now by the infestation of man.
The dregs of society
Abandoned and reduced to scavenging within a twilight world,
Stained by neglect, centuries in the making.

M. Krochmalnik Grabois

Huckleberries

This couple
they were high school sweethearts
He was half man/half dog
more wolf really
she half reptile/half bird
the plumed serpent
in the big-breasted, leather-clad flesh

On prom night he put his hairy head
into the punch bowl
She slithered across the dessert table
like an iguana
her tail flicking aside
tortes and meringue

They'd been watching the movie *Carrie*
in preparation for the big event
but there was no correlation
No one would dare bully
or ridicule them

After promming off
they smoked dope

(Continued on page 28)

in the house of the dwarves
Every one of them had lost their virginity
by the age of fourteen

They loved getting it on with dwarves
Fidelity was nothing
they valued
nothing the dwarves valued
They would kill anyone who would take
what was theirs

Their garage breathed in and out
like a cartoon garage
crazy clarinet riffs
their ongoing soundtrack

Then they left the dwarves
to do what dwarves do after events
that are allegedly life-changing

and rode rusted-out dirt bikes into the Mojave
to celebrate their Mayan heritage
til the sun came up
then set the bikes down in the cool, exhausted sand

rolled over and worshipped
the Rabbit in the Moon
got on their knees

flaaagellaaated themselves like Spanish priests

pounded their foreheads with
chunks of jade with 400-million-year half-lives
royal jade
orange flecked with green

blood spots on their foreheads
the sheriff's squad car
roiling up the dust in the distance

I'll be your Huckleberry, said Man/Dog
I'll be yours, said Bird/Reptile

They were ready to move on

donnarkevic

I Cannot Remember

the name of that boy in first grade
who sat in front of me
who was hit by a steel truck,
his closed coffin small as a pencil box.

Classmates stood in neat rows
like Crayolas, all black,
how his mother cried like the Pieta,
his father standing with the men
stiff on whiskey, the undertaker
telling dirty jokes to the priest.

For the rest of the school year
no one sat in his chair.
When we passed papers to the front,
I stretched over the vacant space
like reaching out for God,
only to find him absent.

Hal O'Leary

My Commencement Speech

On this your day you will receive
advice from everyone you know.
There's little of it you'll retain
And really there's no reason why you should,
for what you will most likely get
are all the things that brought success to them,
as though your life should be a mirror of their own.

But who knows what your life will be,
what opportunities you'll find,
what trials you may encounter.
Just be prepared for all that comes your way,
And toward that end take heed of this,
In opting twixt the head and heart,
I'd choose the heart for happiness.
And for success, you need no more than this.
Keep all options open
for as long as well you can.

Alan Catlin

Hanging There on the Wall

The face she was seeing
in the back bar mirror was
something from the Ash Can
school of Art: charcoal and
newsprint smudged, urban
decayed and gray features
down in some Mid-town dream
of Manhattan, collaged by
Rauschenberg, bled on by Pollock
on a dream date with Death.
None of the Art Houses would
have her, not even the nude revues.
She might have been a chorus girl in
once upon a lifetime ago or a stripper,
before her drawn features
became ravaged by close encounters
with designer drugs, speed dialing
Crystal and Mona Lisa martinis
straight up, in twenty dollar a pop
all night lounges she hung out in,
so hung over in sun shining afternoons,
wraparounds can't hide the light.

32

Once outside, her self-portraits
appeared in store front windows
like something painted by Francis Bacon,
with a razor blade and a knife:
viscera, tempura and tender loin
on glass, two drinks and a white
powder blast from being a late
in life model for a Damien Hirst,
sawed in half and preserved in
formaldehyde, floating in a smudged
glass display case.

New to Penny Ante Feud? You'll want to catch up on our back issues:

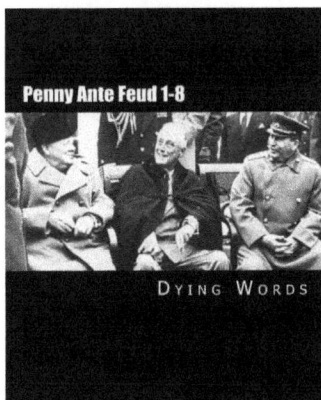
Penny Ante Feud 1-8
DYING WORDS

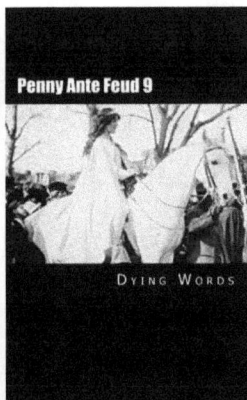
Penny Ante Feud 9
DYING WORDS

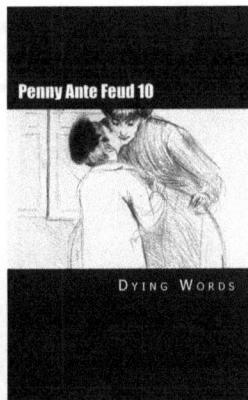
Penny Ante Feud 10
DYING WORDS

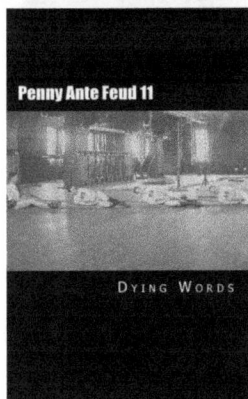
Penny Ante Feud 11
DYING WORDS

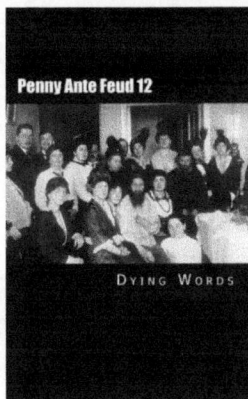
Penny Ante Feud 12
DYING WORDS

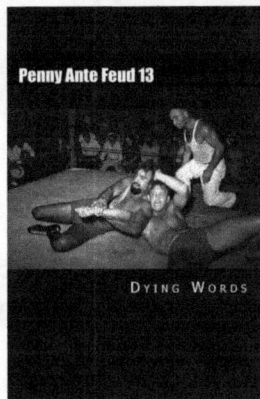
Penny Ante Feud 13
DYING WORDS

Please check our website www.shoemusicpress.com for current pricing (special bulk discount and author pricing available).